I D I O M S

An Amusing Look At American Speech

Anne L'Esperance
Illustrations by Whitney Marie Daley

CAPISTRANO PRESS

Idioms: An Amusing Look At American Speech

Library of Congress Catalog Card No. 90-084630

ISBN: 0-9628506-0-8

First Edition

Printed in the United States of America

Back to the drawing board.

Contents

ACKNOWLEDGEMENTS

This book is dedicated to the memory of my mother, Bernice (Giffels) O'Connor. She was a teacher who inspired hundreds of students. A widow, she raised her four children with love and patience. In spite of many challenges, she lived her life fully, meeting losses and hardships with strength, quiet determination and optimism. I am grateful for her example.

My husband, John, provided encouragement and moral support. Whitney Marie Daley, our daughter, did all the illustrations in this book. Her brother, Guy was the knowledgeable and conscientious art editor.

Copy editors Sarah Peck, Carol Duncanson and Betty Taylor were also generous with their time and expertise. I thank them and, last but not least, I thank Marcy Huber for suggesting that I undertake the task.

INTRODUCTION

The purpose of this book is to eliminate some of the confusion of American speech. Having learned *English,* many newcomers expect to communicate easily, but are soon confronted by conversations such as the following;

I guess we blew it. We expected every Tom, Dick and Harry to go overboard and pay through the nose for our butter cream cookies. But we were barking up the wrong tree. People said they thought the cookies were for the birds.

You're right. We dropped the ball because we didn't have an ear to the ground. We should have known that most people have decided to eat low-fat food. Oh well, let's go back to the drawing board. We'll come up with something that tastes great and our customers will be floored when they find out that it's healthy, too.

We have tried to introduce some of the more commonly used idioms. Each one is explained briefly, and is followed by an example of its use in colloquial American speech.

Since "a picture is worth a thousand words," - and we think these are worth a few laughs as well - the words are kept to a minimum. The illustrations help convey the meanings in a memorable and enjoyable manner.

NOTE: Because we want to use expressions as they are spoken, we have avoided the usual *"one's"* as in "Toot *one's* own horn." Instead we use the words - "your," "our," "his," "her," or "their."

All thumbs.

When people are clumsy, we say that they are "all thumbs."
Everyone likes Al, but he's not very good working with his hands
He seems to be all thumbs.

As the crow flies.

When people say "as the crow flies," they are talking about the most direct route between two places. *The post office is on the other side of the river. It's a three mile drive from here even though it's only a few blocks as the crow flies.*

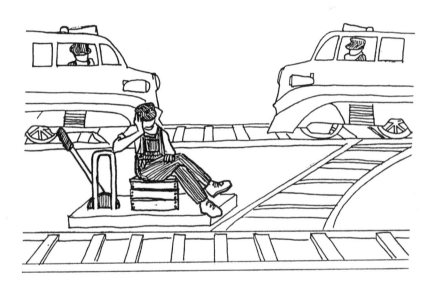

Asleep at the switch.

If someone is "asleep at the switch," they are not paying attention to what is happening. *The light turned green, but the car ahead of us didn't move. I guess the driver was asleep at the switch.*

At the end of your rope.

If you are "at the end of your rope," you have handled as many problems as you can manage. *You have so many responsibilites at home and on your job. You must be at the end of your rope.*

Back to the drawing board.

If something you tried failed, you might say, "Back to the drawing board," even though the ideas or plans never started at a drawing board. *The coach said, "That play didn't work. We'll just have to go back to the drawing board."*

Barking up the wrong tree.

You are "barking up the wrong tree" when you put a lot of effort in the wrong place. *Carlos thinks he will impress Jessie with his new motorcycle, but we think he's barking up the wrong tree.*

Bend over backwards.

When you try very hard to please someone, you bend over backwards. *Bill is always so helpful. He bends over backwards to help his aunt, but she never seems pleased.*

Bent out of shape.

If people feel that they have not been treated very well and they are upset, we say they are bent out of shape. *The repairman was three hours late and Mr. Jones was not a bit happy. He was really bent out of shape.*

Big fish in a small pond.

Someone who is important in a small group but might not have much influence in a larger organization is a "big fish in a small pond." *Our mayor says he wouldn't like to be a congressman in Washington; he'd rather stay here and be a big fish in a small pond.*

Bite the dust.

To "bite the dust" means to lose or to die. *We thought our football team would win the playoff, but they really bit the dust when they lost last weekend.*

Blew it.

If you attempted to do something, but did not succeed, you "blew it." *It was a good meeting until Marvin gave his long speech. He really blew it, because he made people lose interest.*

Bull in a china shop.

A person who is not careful with delicate things or situations is like a "bull in a china shop." *Chuck is such a good baseball player, but I'm surprised that he is also a good jeweler. I thought he'd be like a bull in a china shop.*

Cat got your tongue?

If somebody says, "Has the cat got your tongue?" they are wondering why you have not been talking. *Carl always waits until he is sure everyone has finished speaking before he says anything. Sometimes it seems that the cat has got his tongue.*

Chip on your shoulder.

If you have a "chip on your shoulder," you resent something and stay angry. *Karen is usually a good sport, but she has a chip on her shoulder about the referee's last decision.*

Close shave.

If you had a "close shave," you narrowly missed an accident. *The bridge collapsed just a few seconds after we crossed it. What a close shave!*

Cold feet.

If you have "cold feet," you are afraid to do something.
The dancer had rehearsed for many weeks and knew the dance very well, but when it was time to go on stage she got cold feet.

Cool.

People, especially young people, say that a person or thing they like is "cool." *I asked her if she'd like to go to the game with me and she said, "That's cool." But when I asked if she would like to go to a movie she said, "That would be cool!"*

Different strokes for different folks.

"Different strokes for different folks," means that people make different choices. *Some people like rock concerts, others prefer ballet - different strokes for different folks.*

Don't bug me!

When people say "don't bug me," they mean that they don't want to be disturbed. *Jane is always so serious about her work; you know she doesn't want to be interrupted. Unless something is very important she says, "Don't bug me!"*

Drives me up the wall.

A person or thing that is difficult or troublesome, "drives me up the wall." *Timmy's mother never get's upset, but when I babysit, he really drives me up the wall.*

Drop the ball.

When you "drop the ball," you haven't gotten something done. *Did you remember to mail the check, or did you drop the ball?*

Ear to the ground.

If you have your "ear to the ground," you are watching or listening for a change in a situation. *I don't expect a huge increase in sales, but I am keeping my ear to the ground so that we'll be able to increase production if we need to.*

Early bird gets the worm.

Often the first person to arrive gets what he came to get, so we say that the "early bird gets the worm." *I wasn't at the sale early enough, so I didn't get the best bargains. Next time I'll remember that the early bird gets the worm.*

Easier said than done.

Somebody might talk about a job as though it is easy to do when, in fact, it is "easier said than done." *Some managers ask workers to do things that are not really possible. They forget that some things are easier said than done.*

Eat like a bird.

If you "eat like a bird," you are not eating very much. *I never eat much at one time. I guess you could say that I eat like a bird.*

Eats like a horse.

A person who "eats like a horse" eats a lot. *After playing football all afternoon, Bill said that he could eat like a horse.*

Every Tom, Dick and Harry.

When you talk about every "Tom, Dick and Harry," you mean anybody and everybody. *That isn't so remarkable. Every Tom, Dick and Harry can ride a bike.*

Eyes bigger than stomach.

If you say her "eyes are bigger than her stomach," you mean that she thinks she'll be able to eat more than she can. *Lisa likes dessert and thinks she can finish a big serving, but it seems that her eyes are bigger than her stomach.*

Fish out of water.

If people are in a situation which is unfamiliar and uncomfortable, we say that they are like "fish out of water." *The engineering students didn't enjoy the French cooking class. They felt like fish out of water.*

Fishy.

If something is unusual and suspicious we say that it is "fishy." *Our neighbors are on vacation, but I hear noises coming from their apartment. I think something fishy is going on.*

Flipped their lid.

When somebody is surprised and upset, we might say that they "flipped their lid." *When James told Barbara that he wasn't going to go to college, she flipped her lid.*

Floored.

If something surprised and impressed you, you would be "floored." *When Jill invited me to dinner, I didn't expect such a beautiful setting. I was really floored.*

Fly-by-night.

If something is considered to be "fly-by-night," it is not very dependable. *Even though they had the lowest bid, we won't hire them because we've heard that they are a real fly-by-night organization.*

For the birds.

If you say something is "for the birds," you don't like it.
*Did you see the new statue in the park? I don't like it very
much. I think it's for the birds.*

Get carried away.

If you "get carried away" with something, you don't
know when to stop. *Mr. Smith is always nervous when his
wife takes her credit card to the mall. She loves to shop and
sometimes she gets carried away.*

Get off my back.

When someone says "get off my back," they are tired of being told what to do. *I wish my neighbor would quit telling me how to do everything. If he doesn't, I'll have to tell him to just get off my back.*

Get the picture?

Someone saying, "Get the picture?" wants to know if you understand what has been explained. *The guide politely explained the plans for the day. But we thought he sounded a little rude when he said, "Get the picture?"*

Give me a hand.

When people say, "give me a hand," they mean they want your help. *If we are going to meet the deadline, we will have to ask a lot of people to give us a hand.*

Go to the dogs.

When things are not maintained very well, they "go to the dogs." *That building hasn't been taken care of for a long time. The owners have just let it go to the dogs.*

Going overboard.

If you "go overboard," you do something to excess. *Joe always likes to decorate the boat for parties, but it looks like he went overboard this time.*

Going through the motions.

When people "go through the motions," they look like they are getting something done, but they are not doing anything. *It seems that we have to look busy even when there is not much to do. So we shuffle papers, just going through the motions.*

Hang in there.

When you "hang in there," you stay with something even though it is difficult. *Some days we are much too busy at the office, but I hang in there because I really do like my job.*

Have your cake and eat it too.

When you "have your cake and eat it too," you have all the advantages and none of the disadvantages. *Mike thinks he can spend a lot of time watching television instead of studying and still be on the honor roll. He wants to have his cake and eat it too.*

Head for the hills.

When people are in a hurry to escape a bad situation, they might "head for the hills." *When his customers realized that he was selling a lot of worthless remedies, Doctor Feelgood decided to head for the hills.*

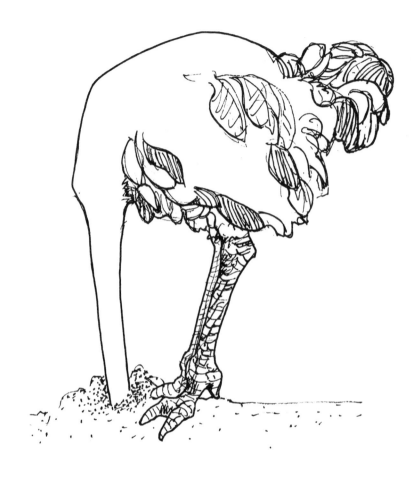

Head in the sand.

If you have your "head in the sand," you refuse to see a problem. *Even though the gymnastics competition is only a week away and she is five pounds overweight, Nellie is still eating ice cream. She has her head in the sand.*

Hit the ceiling.

If you lose your temper, you "hit the ceiling." *When my father saw the phone bill, he hit the ceiling. I was surprised to see him so angry.*

Hit the hay.

When you're tired and you go to bed, you "hit the hay."
It's past my bedtime and I'm tired, so I'm going to hit the hay.

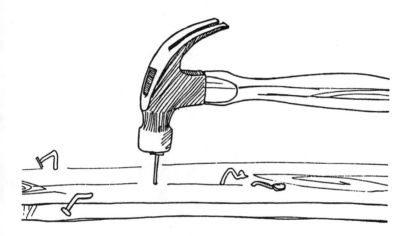

Hit the nail on the head.

If you are very accurate about something, you "hit the nail on the head." *When her counselor told her she had the potential for becoming a good doctor, he hit the nail on the head.*

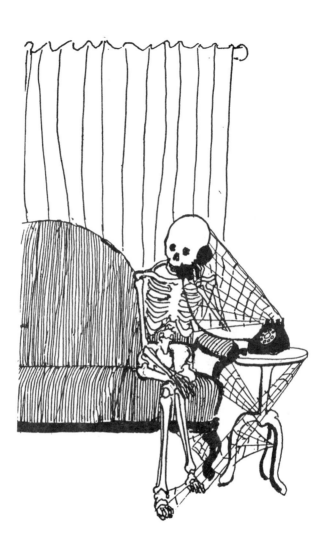

Hold.

If you are talking on the phone and someone asks you to "hold," they want you to wait because they have to leave the phone for a short time. Being "on hold" means to be waiting. *I couldn't get much done this morning. Every time I tried to make a call I was put on hold.*

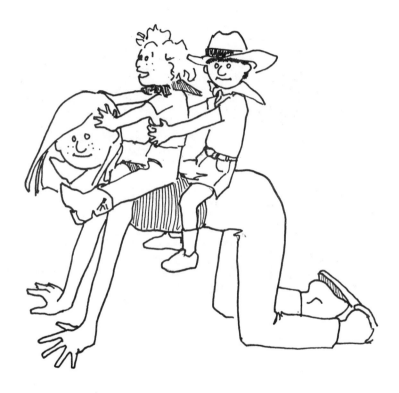

Horsing around.

"Horsing around" means playing actively or recklessly. *Terry was told to quick horsing around on the diving board because he could injure himself or another swimmer.*

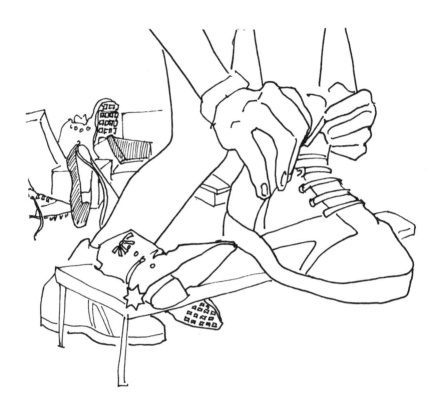

If the shoe fits, wear it.

If something seems appropriate for you, someone might say, 'if the shoe fits, wear it.' *My teacher said that I should study bookkeeping instead of secretarial work. She told me to focus on what I do best. She said, "If the shoe fits, wear it."*

Job is on the line.

If you are at risk of losing your job, your "job is on the line." *Bret is being very careful at work. He was told that if he made any more mistakes his job would be on the line.*

Keep a lid on it.

If you "keep a lid on it," you keep it secret. *When I told Marge that we might be moving, I asked her to keep a lid on it because we don't want anyone else to know our plans.*

Knock on wood.

If you are superstitious, you might "knock on wood"
because you think it could make a particular thing
happen. *We probably won't get a good rainfall this year, but
let's knock on wood that we'll get more rain than the weather-
man has predicted.*

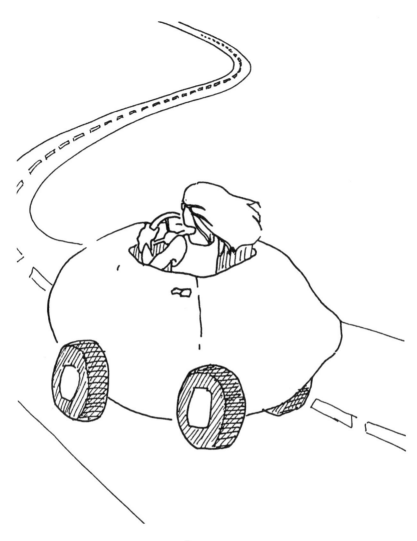

Lemon.

When you say that something is a "lemon," you mean that it doesn't work well. *Michiko likes her new car, but her husband doesn't think it runs very well. He says she got a lemon.*

Let the cat out of the bag.

If you reveal a secret, you "let the cat out of the bag." *We were going to keep the party a secret, but Tony told all his friends. He let the cat out of the bag.*

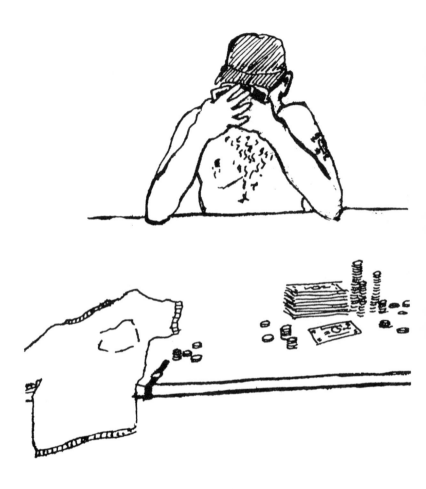

Lose your shirt.

If you "lose your shirt," you lose everything. *Henry invested all his money in the business that failed. He lost his shirt.*

Lying down on the job.

If you aren't doing your work, you're "lying down on the
job." *Fleetfeet used to be a good race horse, but now he's lying
down on the job.*

Make waves.

When you "make waves," you cause problems. *The new director is planning to make a lot of changes in the program. We think he'll make waves for the whole department.*

Money burns a hole in his pocket.

If you spend your money as soon as you get it, we might say that "money burns a hole in your pocket." *As soon as Richard gets paid, he goes on a spending spree. Money burns a hole in his pocket.*

Needle in a hay stack.

When something is impossible to find it is a "needle in a haystack." *He is wasting his time trying to find the little piece of onion in the celery soup. It's like trying to find a needle in a haystack.*

Nose out of joint.

If you feel that you were treated unfairly, your "nose is out of joint." *Barbara is very upset about not getting the promotion. Her nose is "out of joint."*

Nosey.

"Nosey" people want to know about things that shouldn't concern them. *Bob and Marcie wanted to have a private conversation, but the woman at the next table was so nosey. She tried to hear every word that was said.*

Not a leg to stand on.

When someone doesn't have a "leg to stand on," he can't prove that he is not guilty. *He says that he is innocent, but there is proof that he's guilty. He hasn't got a leg to stand on.*

Old hat.

When people are tired of something that has been around a long time, they say that it is "old hat." *The children were amused by the magician, but their grandmother had seen the tricks many times before. She thought the show was old hat.*

On a roll.

When you are "on a roll" you are being very successful with whatever you are doing. *Jeff is doing well explaining the benefits of video promotion. He sure is on a roll. He's making a sale every time he calls on a customer.*

On cloud nine.

If you are on cloud nine, you are very, very happy. *Gene and Lois are so happy making plans for their wedding. They're on cloud nine.*

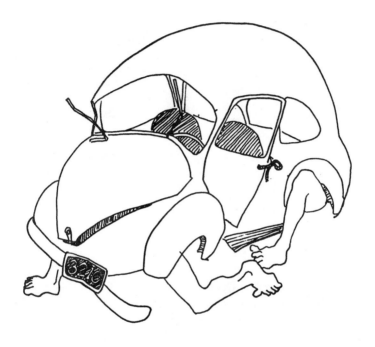

On its last legs.

When a thing is "on its last legs," it's falling apart. *Whitney and Jim will be glad when they get another car. Their old Volkswagen is on its last legs.*

On the ball.

A person who is "on the ball" is very competent and is doing a good job. *Charlene is such a good secretary. She is always on the ball. Everybody is impressed with her good work.*

On the fence.

When someone is "on the fence," they are not taking a stand on an issue. *Her neighbors disagree about the environmental proposition, but Betty is on the fence. She hasn't decided how to vote on it.*

On your toes.

If you are "on your toes," you are aware of all that needs to be done, and you are doing your work well. *Barry is a good bus boy. He is always on his toes.*

Out of the frying pan into the fire.

If someone gets out of one difficult situation only to get into a more difficult one, the person is "out of the frying pan and into the fire." *Kay thought she would have time to volunteer at school because she had finished her work with the Boy Scouts. But now she is busier than ever - out of the frying pan and into the fire.*

Out on a limb.

If you are "out on a limb," you are in a dangerous position. *I know that hiking alone in the mountains can be risky, but I think I'll go out on a limb and give it a try.*

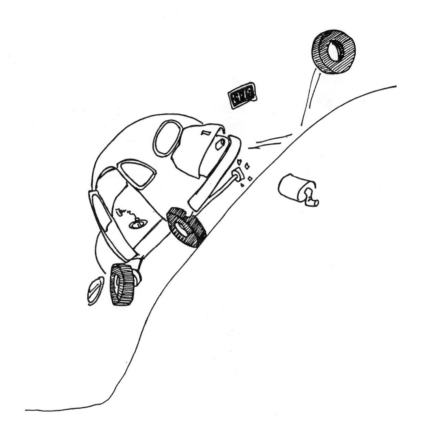

Over the hill.

When people or things are old or worn out, we say that they are "over the hill." *That old car has too many things that need to be repaired. It's really over the hill.*

Paint the town.

When people say that they are going to "paint the town,"
they mean they are going out to have a good time. *It's a
big promotion so we're going to celebrate in a big way. We're
going to paint the town tonight.*

Pay through the nose.

If something is overpriced, you "pay through the nose"
for it. *The new market is beautiful and full of wonderful
things, but they are too expensive. You pay through the nose
when you shop there.*

Piece of cake.

If something is a "piece of cake," it is easy to do. *Have you ever seen Bill roller skating? He's great and he makes it look so easy. You'd think it was a piece of cake to skate the way he does.*

Play it by ear.

When you "play it by ear," you do something without a plan or instructions. *We don't have to make a lot of plans for our trip. We could just play it by ear, checking out the hotels and places of interest after we arrive.*

Pulling my leg.

If you are "pulling my leg," you're fooling me or teasing me. *Did you really grow a five pound tomato or are you just pulling my leg?*

Put your foot in your mouth.

When you say something that gets you in trouble, you "put your foot in your mouth." *I think Wendy was beginning to like you, but you sure said the wrong thing when you told her she was getting fat. You really put your foot in your mouth.*

Raining cats and dogs.

When people say that it is "raining cats and dogs," they mean that it is raining very hard. *We'll have to be careful driving home tonight. It's raining cats and dogs.*

Ruffled feathers.

Hurt feelings are called "ruffled feathers." *The company is looking for a new personnel director. They hope to find someone who won't ruffle any feathers.*

Sell yourself short.

If you "sell yourself short," you underestimate your own value or importance. *You are learning to speak English so well and you have always been a good worker. Don't sell yourself short when you're looking for work. You should be able to get a job that pays well.*

Shape up or ship out.

If someone is told to "shape up or ship out," he needs to improve the way he does things. *Tom has been careless lately and his supervisor told him that he had to shape up or ship out.*

Smell a rat.

If you "smell a rat," you have a feeling that something is not right. *You might think I'm being too suspicious about her story, but I think I smell a rat.*

Snow job.

When someone gives you a "snow job," he convinces you that something is better than it really is. *The salesman convinced Vinh that he should spend a lot of money for something he didn't need. It was a real snow job.*

Spilled the beans.

If someone "spilled the beans," they let everybody know about something. *The formal announcement won't be made until next week, but someone spilled the beans and now everybody knows about the merger.*

Stick your neck out.

To "stick your neck out" is to do something that is risky. *You could stick your neck out and ask for a raise, but it might be a little risky. Maybe you should wait until your boss has a chance to see what a good job you are doing.*

Straight from the horse's mouth.

If you get information directly from a person who knows about something, you get it "straight from the horse's mouth." *Juan is sure they won't raise the rent, because he discussed it with the landlord. He got it straight from the horse's mouth.*

Take the bull by the horns.

When you do something that needs to be done, even though it is difficult or dangerous, you "take the bull by the horns." *We haven't been saving any money lately. Maybe we should take the bull by the horns and try to work out a budget.*

Talk through your hat.

If someone talks through their hat, they are talking as though they know a lot about something when they really are not knowledgeable. *We get a little tired of listening to Pete talk about things he doesn't know about. Most of the time he just talks through his hat.*

Tall tale.

A "tall tale" is an exaggeration of the truth or a complete falsehood. *Grandpa enjoys telling Billy about his great adventures, but soon Billy will wonder if they aren't a lot of tall tales.*

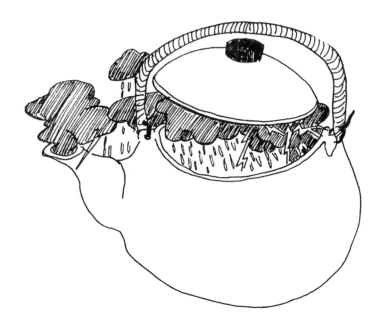

Tempest in a teapot.

When a lot of people get excited about something that is not important, it is called a tempest in a teapot. *The students had planned to protest the new library hours, but they decided it would just be a tempest in a teapot.*

Tenderfoot.

A "tenderfoot" is someone without experience. *Walter took the overseas job even though he wasn't familiar with the area. He said that he knew he was a tenderfoot, but that he would learn from the experience.*

Toot your own horn.

If you "toot your own horn," you tell people how wonderful you are. *Paula has a lot of talent, and she isn't at all modest about it. She likes to toot her own horn.*

Touch base.

When you "touch base" with someone, you keep informed and share information. *Lee was glad that he had touched base with the office. He learned that he had a new customer.*

Turn over a new leaf.

If you "turn over a new leaf," you change bad habits.
Chris used to be late for school every day. but he turned over a
new leaf. He hasn't been late once this semester.

Up the creek.

If someone has gotten into a bad situation and can't seem to find a way out of it, we might say they are up the creek. Sometimes people say "up the creek without a paddle." *When Sam realized his keys were locked in his car he felt that he was up the creek.*

Walk on eggs.

To "walk on eggs" is to be very careful. *We don't relax when we talk with Howard because he often takes offense at innocent remarks. People say you have to walk on eggs when you are with him.*

Wet blanket.

A dull or depressing person is called a "wet blanket."
The other guests were relieved when Art left the party. They
were tired of his long, sad stores. He sure was a wet blanket.

Wolf in sheep's clothing.

A "wolf in sheep's clothing" is someone who is not as trust-worthy as he seems. *The candidate has made some interesting proposals, but some people don't trust him. They think he is a wolf in sheep's clothing.*

I N D E X

INDEX

I N D E X

I N D E X

I N D E X